Poems of Love & Life: Our Courtship in Rhyme

By

Joseph W. Svec III

&

Lidia B. Svec

First edition published in 2021
© Copyright 2021
Joseph W. Svec & Lidia B. Svec

The right of Joseph W. Svec & Lidia B. Svec to be identified as the author of this work has been asserted by him in accordance with the Copyright, Designs and Patents Act 1998.

All rights reserved. No reproduction, copy or transmission of this publication may be made without express prior written permission. No paragraph of this publication may be reproduced, copied or transmitted except with express prior written permission or in accordance with the provisions of the Copyright Act 1956 (as amended). Any person who commits any unauthorised act in relation to this publication may be liable to criminal prosecution and civil claims for damage.

All characters appearing in this work are fictitious. Any resemblance to real persons, living or dead, is purely coincidental. The opinions expressed herein are those of the author and not of MX Publishing.

Paperback ISBN 978-1-78705-946-7
ePub ISBN 978-1-78705-947-4
PDF ISBN 978-1-78705-948-1

Published by MX Publishing
335 Princess Park Manor, Royal Drive,
London, N11 3GX
www.mxpublishing.co.uk

Cover design by Brian Belanger
Internal images by Clipart.com

To

This book is dedicated to you.

May you find true love.

May you experience true love.

May you have everlasting love.

1st Corinthians 13:

"The Greatest of these is Love."

Contents

Introduction

Morning

A Knight's Maiden

Reflections

Morning Passage

Words Alone

In Each Moment

Just Yesterday

Evening Star

Happy Anniversary

The Toy Shop

A Portrait of Lee

When I look into Your Eyes

Enchantment

To my Valentine

Gifts

Happy Anniversary (2008)

Country Cottage

Love Song

Radiant

To Leedjia & Tim, on their Wedding

Where in Your Heart do I Live?

A Time for Us

Sunset Symphony

Every Road it Leads to You

Pixy Muse

April Song

A Voyage to You

Crystal Rainbow

Morning Song

Sunshine and Daisies

In Your Arms

Shall we Dance

In Morning Shadows

Timeless

Farm Birds

I am Thine

Valentine's Day

Crystal Home

Tea in the Gazebo

Teddy Bear's Christmas Tea Party

You Are my Everything

Sparkling

Captain's Cottage

Happy Anniversary (2018)

The Captain's Candy Cane Christmas

When You're Near Me

Dazzling!

My Love is Always with You

Greenhouse Magic

A Stroll in the Garden

My Love

I am Yours

Christmas Magic

To Our Priscilla

You are Everything to Me

Anniversary!

On our Golden Anniversary

Introduction

True love is real. It can happen at any time, or place, and at any age. It can be realized instantly, or it can grow over time from the simplest of beginnings. I would like to share the story of how my wife, and I came to know each other, and came to realize the love that we share.

We met at a public speaking contest, when I was a junior in high school, and she was in elementary school. She had accompanied her older sister to the event. Lidia, or Lee, the nickname she went by, sat next to me on the school bus, and we began talking about life, goals, dreams, society, poetry and other subjects. Over the course of the school year, on the bus rides to and from the public speaking contests, we very much enjoyed our conversations, and the time spent together in friendship. When the school year ended, we exchanged mailing addresses and continued our friendship through letters. Email did not yet exist back then.

We continued writing over the years, and eventually began calling on the telephone, with some of our conversations lasting over three hours. After several years, when I was then in college and she was in high school, I visited her at home, to play guitar and share tea & cakes, and enjoy our conversations in person. We often went for walks in the garden, talking and enjoying the flowers, and each other's company. We had become the very best of friends.

During my junior year in college, I was selected for a study abroad program to spend my senior year at the University of Barcelona, in Spain. It was then, that we realized there would be no more phone calls, or walks in the garden, and Spain was a very long way from the midwestern town in which we lived. We both came to understand just how much we truly meant to each other, and that we did not want to be apart. After some consideration, I withdrew from the year abroad program, and planned to finish my senior year of college locally. We got engaged to be married in one year, when I graduated. At the time of our engagement, we had not yet kissed, or even held hands.

The year prior to our wedding had many challenges, as even though her mother thought highly of me, her father was adamantly against the wedding, and my mother wondered what on earth I was getting into, marrying a girl still in high school! But they did not understand the love and friendship we felt. We were, and still are soulmates. Lidia and I were married on June 10, 1973, the day I graduated college.

Over the years, we have continued to romance and court each other, (or in today's terminology, to date each other), taking time to go to a concert or a local theater production, or to a tea room. We still spend hours and hours talking, sharing our friendship, and just enjoying each other's company.

When asked about the longevity of our relationship, Lidia replies, it is the continued romancing, that keeps it alive and growing, making the other feel truly special. Looks may fade over time, but in love's eyes, beauty is forever.

We are grateful that we got married when we did, and for all the time that we have shared together, but it is not just the quantity of the time, but the quality. Make each moment a unique celebration.

I have always enjoyed writing poetry. In fact, that was one of the things that brought us together initially, when we first met. Over the years, for special occasions, such as Christmas, birthdays, anniversaries, and Valentine's Day, I have written love poems to my wife. And to chronicle special moments or significant events in our lives, I have written narrative story poems. The collection of these poems has become a memoir, a window into our courtship over time.

As we approach our fiftieth wedding anniversary, we have gathered this collection into the book, that you are holding in your hands, "Poems of Love & Life: Our Courtship in Rhyme", and we are happy to share it with you.

Morning

Soft
my drowsy eyes
awake to each new day,
as the sun erases all of last night's sleep away.

Sweet
the morning sings
it's new song to my ears,
as it washes clean the soul of all of last night's fears.

Silver
in the sunlight,
tiny dew drops shine,
making shimmering patterns in a spider web's each line.

Subtle
is in its tininess,
the song a cocoon sings,
will soon burst forth in colors of a butterfly's new wings.

Soft
your drowsy eyes
awake, the new day is adorning,
each new day I wish to you a loving bright "Good morning.

A Knights Maiden

A knight's fair maiden is his strength.
He will go to any length
in all he does, a quest so pure,
driven by his love for her.

You sweet maiden fill my heart
with love so great, that I should start
to glow with radiance of the sun,
brighter far, than anyone.

Though I am fire, you are flame,
burning bright, one in the same.
Brighter than bright shining star,
is the love we share by far.

Your beauty is my eyes delight.
There'll never be another sight.
as precious as my maiden fair,
in silken gown and sun kissed hair.

A rainbow diamond sparkling bright,
you bathe me in a heavenly light,
that guides my path, in all I do.
My life, I live for only you.

I carry as silken scarf, your kiss.
This knight asks of you only this,
your loving thoughts, eternal, true,
forever constant, always new.

You fair maiden are my strength.
I will travel any length
in all I do my quest so true,
is guided by my love for you.

Reflections

You bring sunshine to my springtime,
    and cast a glittering glow,
so subtle in its softness,
    that neither of could know,

the music and warm friendship,
    that we shared throughout the years,
would turn to loving feelings,
    with its happiness and tears.

You bring flowers to my Summer,
    blooms of laughter love and light,
moonlit kisses, deep and warm,
    on a silver summer night.

The magic of the silent forest,
    lives within your eyes.
Your smile is a sparkling rainbow,
    brightening summer skies

The harvest of our Autumn,
    our two children bright and strong,
will live in love we gave them,
    as through life they go along

Child poet, brave adventurer,
    both so loving in their way,
are reflections of the gentleness,
    you impart throughout the day

Though your absence is my Winter,
    with its emptiness and pain,
our love is the sunshine,
    I can see beyond the rain.

When snowy separate paths we walk,
    our hearts are still as one.
Joined forever by the love we share,
    till endless time is done.

You are with me ever always,
    in the passing of each season,
timeless through the years,
    and our love it is the reason.

You bring sunshine to my springtime,
    in the Summer, flowers bright,
that will last through Fall and Winter,
    blooms of laughter love and light.

Morning Passage

Heading out to somewhere neath a starry sky of sea,
heading out away from where I'm longing now to be.
My love lies softly sleeping, neath the starry sky and trees.
My heart lies softly with her, midst the gentle, flowing breeze.

Night to morning gently creeping, through orange, aqua skies,
sparkling stars lie quietly sleeping in her azure eyes.
Feather clouds of golden thread cradle the newborn day.
Feather thoughts of gentle loving cradle her as she lay.

Silently, in silhouettes, the mountains do appear,
clothed in amber satin of the sunrise drawing near.
Clothed in silent slumber and the dawn star's shimmering light,
her beauty is the shimmering jewel, that brings to me delight.

Soft I whisper, "I love you, Lee." in the morning skies.
Sweet the East wind carries to her on the new sunrise
all my thoughts of lovingness, that fill me through the day,
that fills the silent world of my morning passageway.

Words Alone

ABCDEFGHIJK
LMNOPQRST
VUXYZ

Words cannot begin to say
the timeless never-ending way
your magic, warmth, and endless love
warms me, like the sun above.

How could I ever hope to show,
the endless, loving, peace I know,
when in my arms you gently rest?
No words could ere' express it best.

And when I gaze into your eyes,
of sun kissed sparkling, azure skies,
no poem could ever hope to be
all that your love does mean to me.

A thousand loving songs could never
express my love for you forever.
Yet these words I shan't restrain,
for surely, I cannot contain

the fire that so brightly burns
in my heart and longing yearns.
Yes, my heart it longs to be
the one, whose words do comfort thee.

And may your sparkling azure eyes
the fullness of my love surmise,
though these words be just a mirror.
I long that they would draw you nearer.

Nearer, closer than the air,
a loving peace, that we might share,
in world, enchanted, bright and true,
I long that I would shelter you.

Our timeless, never-ending love
would be the sun, so bright above.
Our magic warmth and endless light,
would be the stars, that fill the night.

Though words alone cannot convey
my love for you, this I must say,
through time, and all eternity,
my words of love I'll live for thee.

In Each Moment

Though we may be apart, at times throughout your day,
you are always with me, in every loving way.
In the subtle softness of an amber, gold, sunrise
I feel the gentle sweetness, of your smile in morning skies.

Your laughter's like the tiny flowers dance, of colors bright,
ringing like a crystal song, in sweetness and delight.
The sparkling magic of the stars, glows within your eyes,
lilting like a butterfly, in silver moonlit skies.

Your loving warmth embraces me and touches deep my heart.
You are with me ever always loved. Never shall we part.
And I too, am with you in, each moment of your days.
The gentle breeze, it echoes, "I love you for always."

Golden in the sunlight, silver in the stars,
my love it is a rainbow, that reaches from afar,
to fill your life with colors, warm and tender, ceasing never,
always, in all ways, and loving you forever.

Just Yesterday

Just yesterday, so long ago,
we vowed our love, for all to know,
that you and I, then and forever,
would love each other, ceasing never.

In forests green, midst flowers, bright,
hand in hand, in love's soft light,
we shared our dreams of future life,
I, your husband, you, my wife.

But more than that, we'd be a friend,
to each other, without end.
There to talk, there to hear.
There sooth and calm a fear.

Just yesterday, as we walked
along the shore, and quietly talked,
the warmth I felt in your soft touch,
filled my heart, so very much.

On ocean shores and sandy beaches,
in the mountain's highest reaches,
your sparkling eyes, and smile bright,
have filled my life with love and light.

But more than that, you are my lover.
There could never be another.
Like a brightly burning fire,
you're my truest heart's desire.

Just yesterday, so close we lay
together at the end of day,
my love for you, eternal and true,
proclaimed itself, as born anew.

As in soft, evening shadows mist,
we embraced each other and lovingly kissed.
My heart, with love, is overflowing,
and its true joy is in knowing,

that you're near, and at my side,
my beautiful princess, my loving bride.
Each day we share, it is a treasure,
that I hold precious, beyond measure.

And the treasure that I give to you,
forever timeless, always true,
is all my love, in every way,
forever and always, each new day.

Evening Star

You are my Evening Star at the twilight of the day,
constant ever with me as the day to night gives way.

First light, always brightest in the evening sky,
your love is warm and guiding when the night is drawing nigh.

No other star could shine the way you sparkle in the night.
They pale before the radiance of your endless magic light.

Endless is the love and warmth, I feel within your smile.
Magic is the moment, resting in your arms a while.

When night is almost over and the dawn sky's growing clear,
you are my radiant Morning Star, whose light is ever near.

When golden soft sunlight gently paints the azure skies,
the Morning Star, so bright and clear, caresses soft, my eyes.

The dawn star is the final star, that lingers into day.
It is a beacon in the East, that shines upon my way.

Always you are with me, in all things that I do,
as eternally, my love is with you, endless, ever true.

Your love it fills my heart by day, is with me through the night.
You are my Dawn and Evening Star, ever burning bright.

Happy Anniversary

My Dearest Lee,

As I reflect upon our wedding, so many years ago,
it seems just yesterday; we vowed our love for all to know.
We were best of friends, so very much in love,
our joy it filled the world, and it lit the sky above.

We climbed the snowy mountains and sailed the crystal sea.
In a world of our own with you, is where I long to be.
You are my inspiration, my friend, my everything.
It is to you alone with love, my heart does always sing.

My thoughts are ever with you, morning, noon, and night.
In my heart, I do embrace you, shining, sparkling, bright.
You are my one warm radiant sun, throughout all the day.
You are my magic evening star, when the darkness lay.

Magic is the moment, when I hold you close to me.
I am yours forevermore, throughout times eternally.
I know my love, that there can never be another you.
Then and now, and every day my love for you is true.

Thank you dear, for all you are, each day of my life.
You're my best friend, my muse, my love, and my loving wife.
Mother of our children two, you are my soulmate, Lee,
I wish with all my love, Happy Anniversary

The Toy Shop

"Where does the magic lay
in the bustle of the day?"
Sighed the toy shop owner, when
two gentlemen came in just then.

"Like my home in Germany." Said one.
"Like days of old that were quite fun".
"I can't quite place this feeling now,
but I'll remember it somehow."

And then his eyes they grew quite bright,
as he traveled to another night.
Six years old on tippy toes,
gazing at toys through whirling snows.

No cares of work or worry or stress.
Just a wonder, a wish, a hopeful guess.
Which magic toy from that display
would he find on Christmas day?

Each year the magic and the joy,
of his brand-new Christmas toy,
would fill his day with wonder bright,
that lasted long, for many a night.

But children grow and set aside
the sparkle of the yuletide.
They must go fast, much faster now
to do the chores adults know how,

But in that timeless magic store,
he'd found his younger days once more.
He left with sparkling eyes so bright,
and blessed the little shop that night.

And then it was, the owner knew
the magic in the memories grew.
Greater than the toys, within the store,
is the gift of childhood, found once more.

A Portrait of Lee

"Tell me, what she's like?" he said. "Describe her now for me."
"Her portrait I will paint instead." I replied to he.
I closed my eyes just for a while, the colors for to seek.
Then so softly with a smile, these words began to speak.

"Magic in the mountain, mystic by the sea,
a timeless springing fountain, of endless mystery.
Sister to the ancient wood, connected to the Earth,
wellspring of all that's good, a seer's eyes since birth.

All creatures great and small, they know her gentle way.
No fear of her at all, do the wild birds display.
Singer of the dolphin song, in the oceans deep.
Traveler of the journeys long, through the realms of sleep.

Take her hand, she'll lead you on a journey to yourself.
Like a book, she'll read you, this enchanting, charming elf.
Keeper of the key, that unlocks your inner being.
Her azure eyes see beyond the limits of your seeing.

Wisdom of the ancient one, dwells within her sight.
Glittering like a golden sun, is her radiant light.
Her voice so sweet and soft, echoes like a crystal song.
I pause to listen oft' and I yearn to listen long.

Her many facets glisten, rainbow colors in the air.
In the silence listen! There was never one so rare.
Her beauty is forever. With one look she can beguile.
Her charm it ceases never, dancing in her sparkling smile.

Enchanted by her spell, in her arms I long to be,
and with her long to dwell throughout all eternity."
Then I took one step aside, the portrait for to see.
A portrait of my loving bride, A Portrait of Lee.

When I Look into Your Eyes

When I look into your eyes, of endless azure blue,
as sunlit summer morning skies, I see each time anew,
the warmth of golden summer days, caressing me so soft,
radiant, amber aqua rays, streaming from aloft.

When I look into your eyes, of crystal, sparkling bright
as star filled autumn, evening skies, you bring to me delight.
Autumn nights so cool & clear, 'neath silver moonlit sky
draw us both so very near, as in our arms we lie.

When I look into your eyes, of deepest aqua, blue
as frozen winter twilight skies, I know that it is true.
The icy cold of winter days melts before your smile.
Your enchanting, loving gaze, warms me for a while.

When I look into your eyes, of shimmering sapphires bright
as springtime's glistening rainbow skies, you are a magic sight.
Like pixies dancing in spring air, playful yet so teasing,
you weave a wondrous path, so rare, ever always pleasing.

When I look into your eyes, of radiant endless love,
the brilliance of the starry skies, smiles with us above.
In your azure eyes forever, always will I see,
our timeless love ceasing never, through all eternity.

Enchantment

Sky and sea so different, are as night and day.
We were told, "Choose your path. There only is one way."
Traveling oe'r an ocean path, the sea would be my bride,
I looked not for another soul. Alone I would abide.

To the sky your path was set, as if cast in stone.
"Don't ask why." You were told. "You'll do this alone."
But then one magic day, in horizon, amber, blue,
Golden sun met silver sea, when I first saw you.

Young in age, you were then no more than just a child.
Still a sage, so wise you were, and I was beguiled.
Sparkling eyes of amber, blue much deeper than the sea,
Where in lies the endless magic drawing me to thee.

Many a day we shared our thoughts on God, and life and more.
Who could say the poems and songs would be a beckoning door?
Through the years we grew and talked, came to be best friend.
Smiles and tears we shared and yearned for it to never end.

Thoughts of you they filled my day, from dawning until late.
It is true I realized; you are my soulmate.
Can it be, this pixy princess, longs to be my wife?
Eternity and longer, I will share with you, my life.

How can I explain the precious love that we do share?
Sea and sky together, dance as one, in rainbow fair.
I love you eternal, through all ages, ceasing never.
I give to you all my love, always in all ways, forever.

To my Valentine

If this Valentine could speak,
loudly, boldly yet still meek,
what is it, it would share?
My everlasting love for you,
eternal, endless, yes and true
it surely would declare.

If this valentine could sing,
it's crystal voice to softly ring,
what song would you hear?
A song of joy, of life and love,
far brighter than the stars above,
a song of you my dear.

If this valentine could dance,
 if it had just one chance,
what is it you would see?
A dance of passion, grace and fire,
pure romance and desire,
all feelings within me.

If this valentine could paint,
 a portrait ever oh, so quaint,
what colors would ring true?
A radiant crystal rainbow bright,
sparkling, shimmering in soft light,
a portrait, yes of you.

If this valentine could fly,
far above the evening sky,
with what would it return?
A strand of silver moonlight soft,
golden stardust from aloft,
all mysteries to learn.

If this valentine could write,
 a poem of lasting love and light,
what verses would it share?
A message from my heart to you,
timeless, yet each day, a new,
my love, it would declare.

Gifts

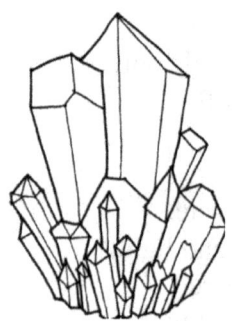

Multifaceted gem, so rare
from ancient mystic time,
sparkling in the morning air,
one look, I know that I am

enchanted, yes forevermore.
I am yours you'll see.
From ancient timeless days of yore,
I'm yours eternally.

Pixie princess, timeless one,
eyes deeper than the night,
yet sparkling brighter than the sun,
forever is your light.

You draw me deep into your gaze,
radiant and soft.
There I will remain for days
and long to linger oft.

One with ocean, sea and sky,
the haunting, sirens song,
you softly sing and draw me nigh.
It sweetly echoes long.

Like the ocean's endless lure,
that beckons one to sea,
your voice, alluring it is sure,
forever calls to me.

On the mountains snowy peak,
you find an inner peace.
In the forest green you seek
a joy that does not cease.

One with nature since a child,
your gifts are rare it's true.
I am enamored and beguiled,
and so, in love with you.

 Canine sprits tame and wild,
in you fully trust.
In your gaze they're but a child,
and follow, you they must.

Oe'r the years you draw them near.
They're always by your side,
For they'll always hold you dear,
and in your love abide.

So many gifts you bring to me,
in your love each day.
What gift can I bring to thee?
What words can I say?

All I am, and ere shall be,
my very being, it's true.
All my love eternally,
this, I give to you.

Happy Anniversary (2008)

"What is love?" one may ask.
A radiance in which we bask.
A warm glow, shining deep within.
A light, that never will grow dim.

Neath the golden new day sun,
a knowing sense of being one,
with a special, magic soul.
To love you always, is my goal.

Long ago you came to me,
and in our friendship, we could see,
a special bond, that we do share,
would keep us close, no matter where

our lives would travel, or would go,
for we are one, in heart, I know.
So came the day, we joined in love,
and were blessed by God, above

I, your husband, you, my bride,
in love and light, we do abide,
celebrating every day,
in every loving, caring way.

You, to me are everything.
In joy eternal, I do sing.
I love you always, my dear Lee,
Happy Anniversary!

Country Cottage

Lilac blossoms in the spring,
so fragrant, sweet and soft,
subtle is the song they sing,
neath verdant trees aloft.

Playful daisies, gold and white,
in clusters here and there,
make for such a joyous sight,
in the summer air.

Roses beautiful and bright,
in every rainbow hue,
fill the garden with delight,
and gently beckon you,

down quiet paths, that wind and wander
past flower, vine, and tree.
Stop a moment just to ponder.
Surely you will see,

Hummingbirds. Their colors glisten,
robins of bright red,
bluebirds, hear their song. Now listen,
singing overhead.

Come inside the cottage door.
Sit here by the fire.
Share a cup of tea or more.
What is your desire?

Linger for a little while.
Leave the world behind.
Let your soul relax and smile.
Feel the peace of mind.

Love Song

I'll sing to you a song of love,
radiant as the sky above,
every note, so crystal clear,
sung to you, alone my dear.

I'll sing the mountains tall and strong.
Granite halls will echo long.
In towering peaks, of ice and snow,
my song of love will live and grow.

I'll sing the forest, ever green.
So sweet a tune, t'was never seen.
Every branch, and leaf, and vine,
will celebrate the love, that's mine.

I'll sing the ocean, azure blue,
Eternal, as my love for you.
Boundless, flowing deep, the tide
my love for you, could never hide.

I'll sing a whisper in the breeze,
that gently touches all it sees,
that lifts my song, upon the air,
to paint in song, your beauty fair.

I'll sing the stars across the sky,
a joyous song, of love on high,
each sparkling, dancing song of light,
a beacon, shining in the night.

I'll sing the silver, silent moon,
a quiet song, a gentle tune.
I'll sing the golden sun, so bright.
I'll sing your love, with all my might.

I'll sing creation, every day,
my love to you, in every way,
reflected in all that I do.
A song of love, I sing to you.

Radiant

In silent darkness of the night,
before dawn does appear,
in sleep you are a gentle light.
I long to draw you near.

Your morning light is sweet and soft,
warm in every way.
In your arms I linger oft',
before we start the day.

Radiant is your smile's light.
It touches soft my heart.
My prayer each day, is that we might
never be apart.

So deep's the light in your soft eyes,
of endless sapphire blue,
one could never full surmise,
the magic that is you.

In your heart, a light does glow,
that pales the noon day sun.
And my heart is yours, you know.
Forever we are one.

Flowers bloom with blossoms bright,
when touched by your hand.
You impart a loving light,
that nurtures all the land.

In orange, azure shadows long,
when the night does fall,
your light is an enchanting song.
Timeless is its call.

Beneath the silver, silent moon,
your light will ever glisten.
Your song's a mesmerizing tune;
my heart, it longs to listen.

By sparkling day, or shimmering night
so radiant you shine.
Your love's a beacon burning bright,
that leads my heart to thine.

To Leedjia & Tim on their Wedding

Love it is an endless song,
Two voices joined as one,
bringing joy, your whole life long,
till endless time is done.

Love it is a melody,
each note and string in tune,
gently played in harmony,
beneath the summer moon.

Love's song is a crystal chord,
pure, and sweet, and bright,
played to each other, each adored
on stary autumn night.

Love's song is a longing gaze,
into each other's eyes
Soft and warm, all through the days,
of snowy winter skies.

Love's song is a gentle kiss.
It's two hearts joined as one,
sharing moments, such as this,
'neath sparking, springtime sun.

Love it is a shining star,
a beacon, bright and true,
leading two hearts from afar,
to find one love, anew.

Love it is an endless song,
a blessing shared by two,
sung each day, your whole life long,
as God smiles down on you.

Where in Your Heart

Where my love, in your heart do I live?
I wonder, as my love, I give.
Your heart's I know a many-faceted jewel.
I could not be but a fool,
to think each room that I could I fill.
So, tell me my love, please if you will.

Am I locked away, in a safe, secret place,
as lovingly, we two are locked in embrace?
Kept safe and protected as valuable treasure,
Guarded securely with every measure?
That would be good, I am quite sure of this,
But are locked away treasures really much bliss?

To be the warm fire in your heart's living room,
where you snuggle up close, to keep away gloom
would give me great joy and be sheer delight.
My loves flame would truly always burn bright.
But fires burn low, and someday are spent.
Where would I be, if the fire, out went?

Could it be true? I'd never have guessed.
But if I could be, I'd be surely blessed.
I'll be bright sunshine that warms every day
Touches you always, in all loving ways.
I'd bathe you in golden glow love, so divine.
But wait! What about the nighttime?

I'd never want to live in a way, so divided.
To not see you for so long, I could not have abided.
But the sun is a star, and stars shine at night.
I'll be your own star shining always so bright.
Your own distant star… No! This wouldn't do.
I could never bear to be so far from you.

My want to fill all your hearts need is real,
Yet I know there are times that I feel,
when my love's failed you (these times I regret.)
I'm cold shivering outside, longing to be let
into your heart, again to be one
who's your treasure, your fire, your stars and your sun.

I long to be held. so secure in your heart,
To love you forever, be never apart.
To be always constant, yet ever new,
And lovingly always be right there for you.
Where in your heart, am I living right now?
Don't tell me… In your smile, I'll see, and I'll know somehow.

A Time for Us

A time for us, so long ago,
we vowed our love for all to know.
Down the aisle side by side,
I your husband, you my bride.

My friend and soulmate ever true,
I longed to always be with you.
And that longing wish came true,
when I was blessed to marry you.

What would the future, for us hold?
Moon of silver, sun of gold.
Nothing mattered more than this,
to love you, hold you, and to kiss

you every day, forever more.
In loving ecstasy we soar.
To start each day with you, my dear,
to hold you close, and feel you near,

it is heaven pure and true,
being blessed to be with you.
You are everything to me.
I pray that in these words you see,

my love for you will never end.
You're my soulmate, bride, and friend.
A time for us we celebrate
on this very special date

So long ago, yet every day,
in each moment, in each way
Forever and always, it is true
I vow my endless love for you.

Sunset Symphony

The afternoon is nearly ended.
Soft twilight has now descended.
City lights as diamonds bright,
are sparkling, glittering in the night.

Silhouettes of mountains tall,
cast their shadows over all,
neath soft, orange glow, of sunset skies,
where radiance in beauty lies.

Subtle is the sweet, sky song.
Each crystal note it echoes long,
a brush stroke of the Master's hand,
painting music oer' the land.

In visual symphony of light,
my soul and senses now take flight.
So filled am I, with awe and wonder,
that all boundaries fall asunder,

and were I to reach inside
to where my heart and soul abide,
and lightly tap my inner being,
it would ring out, clearly seeing

a heartfelt sunset crystal song
that echoes softly, lingers long;
mingles with the symphony,
joins as one and finally

in silence of a dreamless sleep,
so quiet, still and endless deep,
settles as words, beneath my pen,
a poem to sing once more again.

Though sun has set, and day is through,
the symphony is played anew,
each time the poem is read or sung,
a timeless echo clearly rung.

Though the poem pales to compare
with sunset symphony so rare,
it is a simple gift of love
to the Master up above,

to thank Him for the setting sun,
for stars, at night when day is done,
for music, poems, and especially
my wife and soul mate, my bride, Lee.

Many are my blessings true,
and within each day anew,
I look to you, love, by my side
and celebrate the morning tide.

I thank you Lee, for being here,
for loving me and being near.
I give to you my heart and being,
so that in my words is seeing,

the happiness that you do bring,
the songs of love and life I sing.
To know that you do love me too,
is joy and peace each day anew.

Every Road it Leads to You

Every road it leads to you,
no matter where it goes.
This is certain. This is true.
My deepest heart it knows.

To the mountains frosty air,
to walk in snowy fields
amidst the ancient beauty where.
my heart to you it yields.

To the timeless ocean blue,
and the salt sea air.
My heart it longs to be with you,
and my love you're there.

Within the emerald forest tall,
the silence and the peace,
I hear but one true. endless call.
My love will never cease.

In our travels worldwide,
to places far and near,
I long to feel you by side,
to hold you close my dear.

Like a beacon burning bright,
a compass sure and true,
your love it is an endless light,
leading me to you.

You're ever in my fondest dreams.
You're all my heart's desire.
Every path and way it seems,
it longs to lead me higher.

Higher, deeper, farther too,
I know that it is so.
Every road it leads to you.
This my love I know.

Pixy Muse

You are my inspiration,
This, my love is true.
You fill me with elation.
There is no one, but you.

My Pixy Muse, you guide my hand
in all that I do write.
In magic journeys cross the land,
you bring to me delight.

Each new page that's stark and white
is empty, and so bare.
Your love, it is the warm sunlight
That brings forth colors fair.

You are my golden sun above,
at night, my silver moon.
You fill each day with endless love,
each night a gentle tune.

Endless, mystic starlight, soft,
dances in the sky.
You are my guiding star aloft.
Always, by and by.

You lead me to my higher self,
to all that I can be.
You are my sweet, enchanting elf,
There is no one, but thee.

I am yours, forever always.
My heart, you'll never lose.
Through time eternal's endless days,
you are my Pixy Muse.

April Song

April sings a joyous song,
that echoes all month long.
It sings the morning, clear and bright,
and dances through the night.

It celebrates a special birth,
of magic, light and mirth,
of one so loving, sweet and fair,
enchantment, oh so rare.

You, my sweetheart are the one,
a bright and shining sun,
that warms my heart throughout the day
in every loving way.

The flowers join the chorus too,
to sing this song to you.
Their colors bright do echo clear
this song to you my dear.

Hear the gentle crystal tone,
sung to you alone.
Hear it singing far and near,
for all the Earth to hear.

April is a special time.
The beauty that is thine,
proclaimed in flowers, light & song
it echoes all month long.

And in this song, I sing to you,
my love forever true,
Endless & eternally,
my dear sweet soulmate, Lee.

A Voyage to You

Endless is the ocean blue.
Eternal is the sea.
Timeless is my love for you,
through all eternity.

Clear and crystal are the skies,
most beautiful and bright.
Your magic crystal azure eyes,
they bring to me delight.

Golden is the sun above,
dancing high aloft.
Radiant, your smile my love,
is gentle, sweet, and soft.

Silver is the silent moon,
O'er a diamond sea.
Loving is the silent tune,
that I sing to thee.

Cruising o'er the ocean blue,
sails our Golden ship.
Sweet memories for me and you
on this magic trip.

Voyaging across the sea,
to distant lands afar,
every path it leads to thee.
You are my guiding star.

Endless is the ocean blue.
Eternal is the sea.
Loving is my voyage to you,
my dearest sweetheart, Lee.

Crystal Rainbow

Crystal prism pure and clear,
dancing in the light,
casting rainbows far and near,
brings to me delight.

Violet, red, orange too,
dance upon the wall,
yellow, green and azure blue,
leave smiles where they fall.

A rainbow carousel, it's true,
painted ponies bright,
in every color, shade and hue,
prancing in the night.

Multi-facets, each unique,
when shining in the sun,
cast an aura that I seek,
each and every one.

Yet, the crystal pales my dear,
in your shining light,
when I gaze upon you near,
you bring to me delight.

Your eyes of aqua, azure blue,
so deep, and warm, and bright,
draw me ever close to you,
a magic wondrous sight.

Your soft, sweet lips of sweetest wine
I savor in each kiss,
enchanting, loving and divine,
brings to me such bliss.

Your gifts are many, it is true,
each facet, pure and rare;
each a shimmering rainbow hue,
so beautiful and fair.

Radiant colors up above,
Endless, ceasing never,
Crystal rainbow, my true love,
I am yours forever.

Morning Song

I wake up in the morning soft,
to you, here by my side.
I give thanks to God aloft,
for you, my loving bride.

I feel your warm, and gentle touch,
your body close to mine.
I love you, so very much.
My heart is always thine.

I look into your radiant eyes,
of endless aqua blue,
brighter than the morning skies.
They draw me close to you.

I gaze upon your loving smile
as you look at me,
and long to linger for a while,
for all eternity.

I look upon your auburn hair,
so playful, silky, soft,
as a summer breeze so fair,
and long to kiss you oft.

I think upon the days gone by.
Memories of love.
Countless as a star filled sky,
dancing high above.

I ponder on days yet to be.
Our future, you and I,
in loving joy, and ecstasy,
far wider than the sky.

I gaze upon you lying near
me, here, at my side.
In endless love forever dear,
I always will abide.

Thank you for all that you are,
all that you mean to me,
soulmate, friend, bright shining star,
my dear, sweet loving Lee.

Sunshine and Daisies

"Sunshine & Daisies" you did write,
on your notes to me,
so long ago, in summer's light.
And you signed them, "Lee".

Your sweet and gentle, loving smile,
drew me close to you.
Talking with you, for a while,
very soon I knew,

that you are such a special one,
enchanting without end.
Timeless, magic, playful, fun.
I longed to be your friend.

Endless hours, talking late,
well into the night.
Tea and music, our first date.
Oh, what a delight!

Friends and soulmates, lovers too,
we vowed our love forever.
Husband and wife, united true,
loving, ceasing never.

With a smile, I do find
my thoughts are sweet of thee,
thinking on the notes you signed,
"Sunshine & Daisies, Lee".

In Your Arms

In your arms, my love I feel,
a magic that is truly real.
A radiant warmth, from deep within,
that words could not ere begin,

to describe or share with you,
my endless love, forever true.
Yet my heart it longs to stay
and linger in your arms this day.

To feel you near, and close to me,
to gaze upon you, lovingly.
To feel your gentle, soft caress,
delighting in your tenderness.

Captivating is your glance,
a playful, teasing, loving dance,
that holds me ever always near.
That's where I want to be, my dear.

To hold you close, in my arms too,
that you might feel my love for you.
That you might feel a strength, and peace,
a love that will not ever cease.

In each other's arms my love,
a radiant star from far above,
has come to us, to share its light,
and warm us on, this magic night.

For in your arms eternally,
is where I always long to be,
loving you, ceasing never,
always, in all ways forever.

Shall We Dance?

We'll dance in the silver moonlight,
softly, through the night,
with stars shining ever brightly,
what a wondrous sight!

To hold you close and near to me,
This my love, I see.
I long for you ever nightly,
my dearest sweetheart, Lee.

We'll dance in the sunrise,
soft, the morning skies,
They just are a mirror,
of your azure eyes.

To sing to you, a love song,
all the day, so long
to draw you always nearer,
in my arms, so strong.

We'll dance in the daylight,
Ever crystal bright,
I love you forever.
You are my delight.

To ever, always be with you,
Yes, I know it's true.
You know that I could never
bid to you, adieu.

We'll dance in the evening,
My heart will joyous, sing.
Love, it is the reason.
Let our love always ring.

To love you truly, in each day,
in each word that I say,
Through each and every season,
In every loving way.

In Morning Shadows

A hush is in the room my dear,
a softness, in the air.
In early morning shadows near,
my love you are so fair.

As dawn kissed rainbows dance, and glide
o'er us while you sleep,
you're nestled warm, and close beside
me, in the shadows deep.

I gaze upon your silken hair,
upon your gentle smile.
I savor sweet, this moment there.
My heart, you do beguile.

I long to kiss you tenderly,
to wake you, to the day,
but, my love, I can't, you see,
an inner voice says "nay".

"Just let her sleep in quiet rest,
the day comes all too fast."
So lay your head upon my breast.
and let your slumber last.

In morning shadows, all around,
you're cradled by my love,
till bright, the sunlight does abound,
in crystal skies, above.

Then sweet, your eyes they're opening
to welcome in the day,
as morning shadows dance, and sing
and hurry on their way.

A song is in the room my dear,
floating in the air,
that sings a tune, so crystal clear
of a love so rare.

I am yours, my dear sweet Lee,
all night and all the day,
loving you eternally
in every loving way.

Timeless

Timeless, through the ages, fair,
Love wanders down it's pathways rare,
Until it finds a special two,
in whom there lives a love that's true.

Then, Love stops, to gaze a while,
And with a soft, and gentle smile.
Love blesses them, eternally,
a shining star for all to see.

Friends and soulmates joined as one,
brightly shining, like a sun,
sharing endless love that's true,
timeless, yet forever new.

Through the endless halls of time,
beyond all reason, chance, or rhyme,
we found each other on that day,
magical, in every way.

And that magic sparkles still.
You know that it forever will.
I am yours, as you are mine,
ever always, I am thine.

Thank you, Lee, for all you are,
My sweetheart, soulmate, shining star.
Timeless through the ages true,
forever is my love, for you.

Farm Birds

Farm birds pecking in the lawn,
white & red and golden fawn.
Pecking here, scratching there,
fluttering without a care

Here they come, around your feet,
looking for a tasty treat.
Peeping, Cheeping, loud they sing.
What new munchies did you bring?

Rhodies, Silkies, ducks and geese;
baby chicks, as soft as fleece.
Fun to watch for many hours,
dancing out amongst the flowers.

See them running to and fro.
They're on guard duty you know.
They fiercely watch oer' all the land,
Yet, they will eat right from your hand.

Farm birds here for you my dear,
Delight in all of them so near.
Sweet and gentle, all the while,
Brining you a happy smile.

I am Thine

You are my love, dear. Yes, it's true,
eternal, without end.
There can be no one, but you,
my soulmate, and my friend.

I look into your loving eyes,
so crystal blue, and bright
as twinkling, sunlit morning skies,
that keep away the night.

So radiant is your gentle smile,
It brightens all my days.
I long for just a little while,
to bask within your gaze.

Your voice it is so soft, and fair.
It's silver sweet, entrancing,
captivating and so rare,
you set my soul to dancing.

Your touch, it warms me deep inside
a gentle warming fire,
where endlessly there does abide,
a loving deep desire.

I long to hold you close to me;
closer than the air,
kiss you ever lovingly,
caress your silken hair.

You are my love, and I am thine,
your soulmate, and your friend.
Our love it will forever shine,
Eternal, without end.

Happy Valentine's Day

Happy day to you my love,
Happy always, too!
May the sun shine bright above,
and send its smiles to you.

Happy day of hearts, and flowers,
many colors bright,
to while away the endless hours,
from morning to the night.

Happy day of music soft,
so soothing, sweet, beguiling,
I long to hold you closely oft,
and dance within your smiling.

Happy day of colors fair,
So silky satin fun.
Rainbows in the water rare,
My playful, frolicky one.

Happy day of quiet tea,
to share just you and I.
In the loving moments, we
draw near, as time goes by.

Happy day so close and near,
In each other's arms,
embracing you, my loving dear,
basking in your charms.

Happy day my valentine.
My love. it is forever.
Know that I am truly thine,
Endless, ceasing never.

Crystal Home

Crystal home, so warm and bright,
a beacon shining, in the night.
A dream held close, so very long,
at times, was like a fading song.

Yet, we believed, and then behold!
We found at last, our pot of gold.
A magic place, of dreams come true,
We would make it all anew.

A submarine and tentacles too,
Mermaids and a ceiling blue.
Granite, oak wood, and stained glass,
Copper, cherry, polished brass.

Swarovski crystal chandeliers
Casting rainbows, full of cheers
Relax and rest, stay awhile,
Crystal home will bring a smile.

Romantic, Victorian, Steampunk too,
Perfect then, for me and you.
Crystal home so warm and bright,
Forever blessed, by love, and light.

Tea in the Gazebo

Music soft, and colors bright,
flowers bask in morning light.
Tea and cakes, to share with you,
as we start the day anew.

Sitting neath the chandelier,
gazing at my loving dear,
we share our tea, and loving glances
while a playful sparrow dances.

Lilacs, lilies, roses, too,
a multicolored blossoms hue,
surrounds us, with a fond embrace,
a delicate and dainty lace.

A quiet time for you and I,
above an orange, turquoise sky
celebrates a brand-new day,
as the sparkling dew drops lay,

upon the velvet, roses soft.
The rainbow flowers beckon oft.
and we answer willingly,
the gardens treasures for to see.

A special moment, we do share,
timeless, endless, loving, rare.
Back into a gentler time,
elegant with china fine.

Your loving smile leads me there.
Your radiant beauty, soft and fair,
does enchant me through all time.
I am ever, always thine.

Teddy Bear's Christmas Tea

Teddy Bear was her favorite toy,
binging endless hours of joy.
Tea party fun, for Lee and her friend.
Special moments without end.

"Pass the tea, and cookies too,
Care for cream? Oh, have some do."
A delightful way to spend the day,
magical fun in every way.

But young girls must go off to school.
(It is a rather unpleasant rule.)
So, Teddy Bear sat all day alone,
until at last, she did come home.

And once again, twas time for tea,
Teddy Bear, and best friend, Lee,
Their tea parties were such great fun,
But again, to school she had to run.

Then days grew cold, and nights were long,
Teddy Bear heard a Christmas song.
Yes, it was that time of year,
that fills one with a Christmas cheer.

The tree, and lights, and manger bright
were such a precious, lovely sight.
It came so fast, I can't believe
it was already Christmas Eve!

Just one quick cup of tea to share,
with her very special bear,
Then off to bed, first prayers to say,
for soon, it will be Christmas day.

The house was silent, not a sound,
when Teddy Bear looked up, and found,
a jolly elf in red and white,
with bag of toys. Twas such a sight.

He gazed at Teddy Bear a while,
then towards her room, with merry smile
took from his bag a wooden horse,
to join their tea party, of course.

For Santa knew an extra guest,
for their party, would be best.
A friend for Lee, and Teddy too.
t'was Christmas magic, true and true.

For when she'd be at school, all day,
Teddy and the horse would play,
 to while away the hours long,
 until they heard her happy song.

Then she'd enjoy their tea, and sing.
The happiest of songs would ring.
They'd all recall, with great delight,
Teddy Bear's tea, on Christmas night.

You are my everything

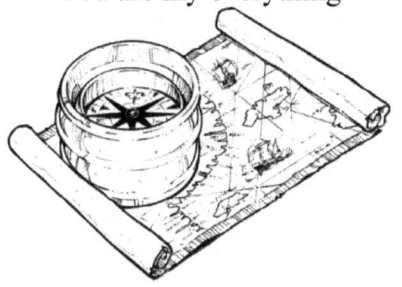

You are my everything, my love,
my bright and sparkling star.
My golden sun, that shines above,
yet never, ever far.

My silver soft, and gentle moon,
casting lustrous beams.
The dulcet, soft, beguiling tune,
that serenades my dreams.

You are my warmth, and comfort pure,
close and by my side.
My steadfast compass, ever sure,
by which I do abide.

My one true soulmate, through all time,
you are the only one.
Always and forever thine,
till endless time is done.

You are my life, my very being.
Each day I will proclaim,
the depth and breath, of my heart's seeing,
an endless, burning flame.

that fills my heart, a beacon bright,
to beckon you by day.
To warm, and comfort you by night,
in every loving way.

You are my everything, it's clear.
There is no one, but you.
I'll be your everything, my dear.
My love for you is true.

Sparkling

Sparkling on a moonlit night,
glistening, in the aire,
twinkling ever always bright,
my dearest love, so fair.

Sparkling is your radiant smile.
You brighten every day.
With soft, sweet charm, you do beguile,
in every loving way.

Sparkling are your azure eyes,
of deep, and endless light.
Brighter, than the aqua skies,
of morning's glorious sight.

Sparkling is your dulcet voice,
so soft, and ever pleasing.
To hear you sing, I do rejoice,
in your playful teasing.

Sparkling is your very being,
in everything you do.
Crystal clear, is the seeing,
knowing it is true.

Sparkling are the Christmas lights.
There's magic in the aire.
It's you who brings the joyous sights,
my dearest, sweetheart, fair.

Sparkling, is my love for you,
shining and aglow,
always, everlasting true.
Eternal, it is so.

Sparkling we do shine as one,
shimmering forever,
Brighter than the brightest sun,
endless, ceasing never.

Happy Anniversary (2018)

Happy Anniversary
my dear, sweet loving bride.
You know I always long to be,
close, and by your side.

To wake up to you snuggled near,
When sunbeams kiss the sky.
To start the day with you, my dear,
as in my arms you lie.

To share each moment, of each day,
Is my heart's desire,
as the golden sun's each ray,
gently reaches higher.

To sail across a sapphire sea.
To softly hold your hand.
To keep you ever close to me,
and journey oer' the land.

To reach our final port, at last,
when soft, the night is due,
our ship of life secure, made fast,
forever, I'll love you.

The Captain's Cottage

A place of quiet, peaceful rest,
a home away from home, and nest.
Drop your anchor here awhile,
and you'll leave with happy smile.

An ocean view, yet miles from shore.
A lighthouse greets you, at the door,
and in each room, you'll find one there
you'll almost taste the salt sea air.

Come inside and sit a spell.
The library has tales, to tell.
A cup of tea will welcome you,
with softly painted seascapes too.

Model ships, of fine detail,
free your thoughts and let them sail,
to a harbor, where its calm.
to rest beneath a shady palm.

The captain and his mate are here,
to welcome you, with hearty cheer.
A cottage filled with God's good grace,
where sun shines through the window lace.

A place of rest, so come ashore.
Look around and explore.
Do drop your anchor here awhile.
You'll surely leave, with happy smile.

The Captain's Candy Cane Christmas

The captain set out from his home, a cottage near the sea.
(Near's a term that for this poem, is perfect, literarily.),
for the seascape, hanging on his wall, was his ocean now.
But he resolved, come calm or squall, to sail again, somehow.

He had heard from a sailor friend, of a magic land,
out beyond the world's end, 't'would be journey grand!
It was, indeed, a magic place, made of candy sweets,
a smile upon every face, and endless tasty treats.

But most of all, he hoped to find the forest, very rare,
Where the branches all were lined with peppermint, so fair.
Yes, candy canes were his delight, so he sailed away,
and journeyed on through dark and light and came to Gum Drop Bay.

Candy Land was true, and real! What a wondrous sight!
Chocolate bon-bons were his meal, on that first magic night.
Then at last he found his goal, the object of his quest.
He knew down deep within his soul; this was the very best.

A forest filled with candy cane trees, so fragrant was the air
Peppermint far as anyone sees. He said a thankful prayer.
He filled his chest with candy canes, and sailed away back home
But crossing oer' the ocean lanes, he heard a woeful moan.

He gazed upon the silver sea. He looked both high and low.
What on Earth now could it be? Very soon he'd know.
A squid appeared not far away, and in a voice so sad,
to the captain, it did say, "Please my dear comrade.

My children all have asked this year, for only, just one thing.
but alas, I truly fear, their sorrowful tears will ring.
Upon the land, I cannot go, to find their hearts desire.
Perhaps by chance, would you know, where I could acquire

candy canes for their one gift? It would be so grand."
The captain's answer was quite swift, and he waved his hand.
"I can help you there, my friend. Do not fret, or fear.
Candy canes to you, I'll send. Their gift, it is right here."

And so, he sent his treasured chest, down, into the sea
Knowing that it would be best. I'm sure you would agree.
The squid with glee, it did reply, "Dear friend, you will be blessed!"
Then winked and waved a sweet goodbye and returned to its nest.

The captain gave a cheerful smile, then to his cottage went.
He did stare for quite a while, when he saw what had been sent.
Candy canes grew from the ground, in a nice straight row.
They twinkled brightly all around, with a sparkling glow.

And each Christmas since that day, the candy canes are there,
to warm the hearts of all that may, see them, oh so fair.
The captain's special candy canes, sparkle through the night
Brightening the winding lanes, with magic and delight.

When you're near me

When you're near me, my sweet love,
your radiance and light,
like the golden sun above,
is gentle, warm, and bright.

When you're near me, warm and bright,
a golden shimmering star,
I know everything is right.
It is the best by far.

When you're near and close to me,
Your warmth, it is such bliss.
To share with you a cup of tea,
a gentle, loving kiss.

When you're near, and loving kiss
me in your arms so soft,
in such endless ecstasy as this,
I long to linger oft.

When you're near, and by my side,
my joy, it is sublime.
In happiness I do abide,
endless through all time.

When you're near me, through all time,
my life, it is complete.
Like a poet's perfect rhyme,
loving, soft, and sweet.

Dazzling!

Dazzling is your smile, my love,
gentle, warm, and bright.
Like the golden sun, above,
you fill each day with light.

Dazzling are your azure eyes.
This my love I know.
Like the shimmering morning skies,
radiant and aglow.

Dazzling is your vibrant aura,
rainbow sweet and soft.
Like the gentle garden flora,
where I linger oft.

Dazzling is your silken hair,
so beautiful, my dear.
Flowing, ever long and fair.
I long to hold you near.

Dazzling is your dulcet voice.
Melodious is your song.
To hear you sing, I do rejoice,
and I listen long.

Dazzling in every way,
my loving sweetheart, Lee.
In each moment of each day,
this you are to me.

My Love is Always with You

My love is always with you,
all throughout your day.
timeless, endless, always true,
in every loving way.

Early in the morning soft,
resting by your side,
I long to linger ever oft,
and in your arms abide.

In the new dawn's morning sun,
I gaze upon my dear.
You're my eternal, only one.
I long to hold you near.

In the afternoon, so bright,
my love is with you still.
a beacon, yes, a shining light,
that ever, always will.

We share a tender cup of tea,
and conversations long.
There can be no one else for me.
Forever is our song.

When the evening comes, my love,
with silver moon lit beams,
shining down from up, above,
you're ever in my dreams.

Through the night, my love is with you.
Know that it is so.
Constant, ceaseless, always true,
as through time we go.

My love is always with you,
all throughout your life.
Enduring, ageless, always true,
my soulmate and my wife.

Greenhouse Magic

Greenhouse magic's everywhere,
from times of ancient past;
in the soil, in the air.
The garden grows so fast.

Tiny seeds are sleeping sound,
Resting through the Winter's night.
Then they wake up in the ground,
to springtime's morning light.

Greenhouse warmth does nurture soft,
while water gives them life.
With gentle rays of sun aloft,
kept safe from stormy strife.

Strong and sound the walls do stand,
whilst wild the wind does blow.
Soon there will be nimzies grand,
sprouting row by row.

Greenhouse magic pure and true
with crystals sparkling bright,
basking in the morning dew,
and the new day's light.

Each day we check with love and care.
We hope they're doing well.
The earthy fragrance in the air,
has timeless tales to tell.

Gardens grand, and woodlands treed,
for eons they do grow.
All started from a little seed,
that God, himself did sow.

Greenhouse magic's all around,
blessing you and I,
bursting forth, from cherished ground,
and sun, and rain, and sky.

Soon our harvest will be here,
as oer our food we'll pray.
And then you and I my dear,
will celebrate the day.

A Stroll in the Garden

Come with me and walk a while.
The garden always brings a smile.
Flowers, veggies, fruit and more,
heirloom rose from days of yore.

Irises in many shades,
grace the garden's peaceful glades.
Lilacs, fragrant, sweet, and soft,
fill the gentle breeze aloft.

Fruit tree's blossoms colors bright,
dance in warm and lilting light.
Soon their tasty harvest fine,
will bring delights that taste divine.

Berries, red and also blue,
are the best. Yes, it is true.
In pies and cakes, or as a treat,
they're wonderful, and oh, so sweet.

The veggies peak above the soil,
rewarding all our happy toil.
Salads fresh, will fill our plate.
So delicious, we can't wait.

The gazebo calls, to sit and rest;
relax within its cozy nest.
The fragrant roses climb and grow.
Up the pillars, watch them go.

Enjoy a steaming cup of tea.
Some tea cakes too, for you & me.
Look, beyond the trellis fair.
Wonderland is waiting there.

Alice, Rabbit, Hatter and Cat
Figs and cherries imagine that.
Joseph's rose, of colors three,
and even Abbey de Cluny.

Take my hand and stroll awhile.
Our garden always brings a smile.
It is blessed by God above,
a place of peace and endless love.

My Love

My Love, she's everything to me,
the sun, the stars, the moon.
A song as endless as the sea,
a mesmerizing tune.

My love, she is my guiding star,
shining ever true.
Her sparkling light is by far,
timeless, ever new.

My love is beauty, sweet and fair,
enchanting and beguiling.
Radiant beyond compare,
she leaves me ever smiling.

My love, she is my world, and more.
Each journey is to her.
She is the ocean and the shore.
Yes, I must concur.

My love she is a gem so bright,
multifaceted and rare.
Her gifts of laughter, love, and light,
are beyond compare.

My love is gentle, soft, and kind,
so caring in her ways.
None like her could I ever find,
searching endless days.

My love is everything to me,
forever without end.
Throughout all eternity,
my soulmate and my friend.

I am Yours

I am yours always, forever,
loving you, ceasing never,
every moment, precious, pure.
Our love is timeless. That is sure.

There can be no one, but you.
My heart is ever always true.
You are my bright and shining light,
your smile such a precious sight.

My love is with you every day,
in every longing, loving way.
Your gentle grace does fill my heart.
I pray that we should never part.

Through time eternal and beyond,
our love it is an endless bond.
I long to hold you close and warm.
We'll be our shelter from the storm.

You fill my days with endless peace.
Our happiness will never cease.
To hold your hand, and feel you near
is such a boundless joy my dear.

Soulmates throughout time enduring,
your sparkling eyes are ere, alluring
Beguiling, yes, enchanting too,
calling, drawing me to you.

Yes, I am yours, throughout all time.
I pray now that my loving rhyme,
can bring to you a happy smile,
forever and an endless while.

Christmas Magic

Feel enchantment in the air,
the sights, and lights, and sounds.
Christmas magic's everywhere.
Enchanting, it abounds.

Each day a gift, a present bright,
a timeless sparkling treasure.
Soft and radiant is the light,
beyond any measure,

Sugar cookies, the best ever,
Hot cocoa, frothy, and fun.,
Oh, can it last, just forever,
or 'till forever's done?

Marzipan and gingerbread,
from Christmas market, grand.
They are the best, it can be said,
the finest in the land.

Soft, the Christmas music rings,
cherished songs of olden,
Carols play, and choir sings.
Their voices, they are golden.

Dance of Sugar Plum Fairy does play,
charming and beguiling.
Captivating in every way,
it always leaves us smiling.

Look now there, around the table,
a shiny new toy train.
Hear its whistle, if you're able,
and bells upon a chain.

Christmas lights in red and green
and sparkling crystal white.
al around they can be seen.
What a wondrous sight!

 Red and golden sunset sky,
dances in the west.
The Christmas Star now draws nigh,
Truly we are blessed.

Come soft the evening, we do share
a cup of eggnog tea.
Another magic moment fair,
I love you, my dear Lee.

You are the greatest gift to me,
in every loving way.
and I am yours eternally,
forever and a day.

To Our Priscilla,
From Mama & Papa Svec

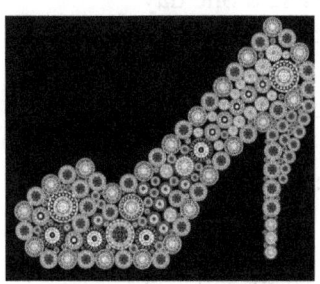

Years ago, just yesterday,
our daughter brought a friend to say.
"I'm Priscilla, how are you?
Leedjia and I are friends. It's true,

we share our shoes, and clothes, and all.
We are in the same dorm hall."
And so began a journey rare,
with this cheerful soul, so fare.

Her laughter, childlike, bright, and soft,
Would echo when she visited oft,
Holidays, occasions too,
she would come, and it is true,

a family member she became,
a daughter in much more than name.
Mama and Papa Svec we were.
That is who we are to her.

The years went by, as they do.
Our children, but of course they grew.
And then our son, he said one day
He loved her more than words could say.

She was a very special one,
who sparkled like a golden sun.
So generous, such a caring heart,
so talented and very smart.

Big eyes that drank in all the world.
reflected love to all unfurled.
So, they were joined as man and wife,
blessed by God for all their life.

Then family times we shared as one,
Tea and cakes, vacation fun,
Whale watching, Disneyland,
Running barefoot in the sand.

Her shoes, amazing, oh so tall.
How could she manage to walk at all?
Even gym shoes were high heeled,
out walking in the pasture field.

But now she walks with God above,
cradled in His endless love.
We may ask, and wonder why
so soon she had to say goodbye,

Her task is done. She gave so much.
With love so many she did touch.
Her organs too, she freely gave,
that other's lives, she could save.

So now we join upon this day,
to celebrate her life, and pray,
Priscilla, thank you, bless you too.
You are a shining angel true.

You Are Everything to Me

You are everything to me,
in every loving way,
sun, moon, earth, sea,
more than words can say.

You are my sun that sparkles bright,
with your warm embrace.
Radiant is your golden light,
shimmering, full of grace.

You are my moon, so silver soft.
Gentle is your being.
A crystal light, that shines aloft,
happiness in seeing.

You are my earth, so full of life,
nurturing, with care.
I am blessed by you, my wife,
in your arms, so fare.

You are my deep enchanting sea,
and I am your shore.
Your loving touch, caressing me,
eternally and more.

You are everything to me,
in every loving way,
and I pray that you can see
in these words, I say,

that there can be no one, but you.
Our love it is forever,
endless, ever always true,
timeless, ceasing never.

Happy Anniversary!

Happy Anniversary,
my dearest, special one.
You are everything to me,
my radiant, golden sun.

You are the warm and sparkling light,
that fills my every day.
And in the quiet of the night,
the star, that guides my way.

You are my soft and silvery moon,
mysterious, beguiling.
The lilting, captivating tune,
that leaves me ever smiling.

You are my timeless, endless sea,
caressing me as shore.
I long to feel you close to me
eternally and more.

You are my soulmate, through all time.
There is no one, but you.
Always, in all ways my love, I'm
certain it is true.

You are truly everything,
more than words can say.
Each day, with love, my heart will sing,
I'm yours, come what may.

Yes, I am yours, my dearest, Lee,
steadfast, ever true.
Happy Anniversary!
Always, I love you.

On our Golden Wedding Anniversary

So many things we've shared as one,
since our wedding day.
Fifty years, so quickly run.
Who knew? Who could say?

Just two youngsters, so in love,
best friends, and soulmates,
asking blessings, from above,
to go forth, to our fates.

O'er the endless ocean, wide,
Off, we sallied away.
Then to the mountains, to abide,
to start a brand-new day.

Sailing, diving, skiing, riding,
so much we did share.
But in truth, there is no hiding,
our love, oh, so rare.

I know there can never be,
anyone like you.
You are everything to me.
Our love is ever true.

Hours sharing cakes, and tea,
lost in conversation,
traveling, just you and me,
all across the nation.

But of all our memories golden,
throughout endless time,
I look back on days of olden,
on our love, sublime.

Our love, it is everything.
Together, our hearts sore.
Endless is the song we sing,
eternally and more.

Thank you love, for all you are,
for everything you do.
You are my true guiding star,
to shine each night anew.

And I long to be the one,
who fills your heart's desire.
To be your bright and golden sun
Your warm and cozy fire.

As we give thanks, a grateful prayer,
for our special day,
to you my loving bride, so fair,
this I long to say,

"Happy Anniversary!
My love ceases never.
For I love you, my dear, Lee,
always and forever".

Also from Joseph Svec III and MX Publishing

Joseph is the author of several Sherlock Holmes stories and novels which can be found at www.mxpublishing.com.

Sherlock Holmes and The Adventure of The Grinning Cat

Sherlock Holmes in The Nautilus Adventure

Sherlock Holmes and The Round Table Adventure

Sherlock Holmes and The Mystery of The First Unicorn

And with Lidia Svec – The Night Before Christmas at 221b, also written in rhymed and metered verse.

MX has published over 500 Sherlock Holmes stories and non-fiction books – and some verse.

Alan Mitchell's Menacing Moors, Menacing Melbournian and Menacing Metropolis are all Holmes stories in verse.

James Moffett, another Holmes author, penned the fascinating Haestingas which is a retelling of the events of 1066 in verse.

www.ingramcontent.com/pod-product-compliance
Lightning Source LLC
Chambersburg PA
CBHW062008070426
42451CB00008BA/293